SECOND EDITION

Workbook **2**

Super Minds

Herbert Puchta · Peter Lewis-Jones · Günter Gerngross · Helen Kidd

CAMBRIDGE
UNIVERSITY PRESS

Contents

Back to school

1 **Look and match.**

wall   board   bookcase   cupboard   door

clock   window   crayon   chair   floor

1 Look, read and tick ☑.

1 There's an apple.   yes ☑   no ☐

2 There's a clock.   yes ☐   no ☐

3 There's a lizard.   yes ☐   no ☐

4 There are some books. yes ☐   no ☐

5 There are some rulers. yes ☐   no ☐

6 There's a board.   yes ☐   no ☐

2 Read and circle.

(1) **There's / There are** a cap on the floor.

(2) **There's / There are** some pictures on the wall.

(3) **There's / There are** a bed by the door.

3 Write about your classroom.

1 There _____ a _____.

2 There _____ some _____.

1 🎧 **001** 🛡 **Can you remember? Listen and write.**

eighty-eight   sixty-six   thirty-three   ~~twenty-two~~

Misty's number's **(1)** _twenty-two_.

You don't see her, but she sees you.

Whisper's number's **(2)** _____.

He can talk to ducks and chicks.

Thunder's number's **(3)** _____.

He can lift a big, big tree.

And Flash's number's **(4)** _____.

She's so fast, she's really great.

2 **Look and match.**

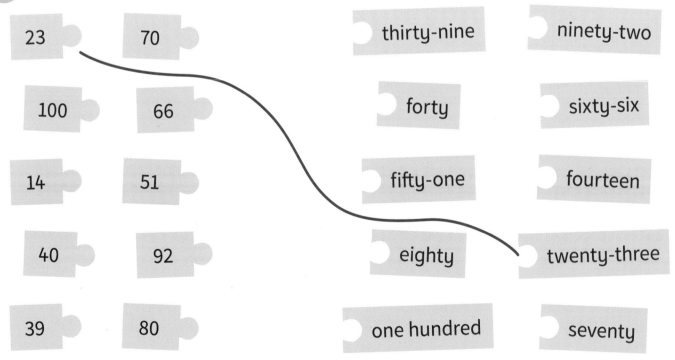

23	70	thirty-nine	ninety-two
100	66	forty	sixty-six
14	51	fifty-one	fourteen
40	92	eighty	twenty-three
39	80	one hundred	seventy

1 Write the words in the correct order.

1 up / Please / stand

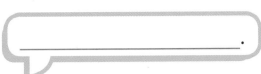
Please stand up .

3 book / your / Open

_____ .

2 sit / Don't / down

_____ .

4 stand / Don't / up

_____ .

2 Look at Activity 1. Number the pictures.

a ☐

b ☐

c ☐

d 1

3 Look and write.

don't   ~~open~~   sit down   stand up

(1) **Open** _____ the book.

Open the book, please.

(2) Stand up. _____, please.

(3) _____ sit down!

(4) Don't _____, please!

Yes!

1 🎧 002 **Who says it? Listen and tick ☑.**

2 🛡 **Look and write the numbers.**

1 I've got an idea. Wait here!

3 Can you check this out, Flash?

2 Great work.

4 We've got them!

a ___

b 1

c ___

d ___

What do I know?

1 Write and circle.

1 I can write the names of five things in a classroom.   **Yes / No**

door _____   _____   _____   _____   _____

2 Which number comes …

after eleven?   _____

after ninety-nine? _____

3 There **is** / **are** some pencils.

2 Look and write the numbers.

1 Please sit down.

2 Don't open your book.

 a

 b

  About me!

3 Read. Then draw and write.

_____

My classroom

29

There is a board.
There are twenty-nine children.

_____
_____

1 Write the words.

~~have~~	brush	get	go
play	go	have	get	have

1 **have** breakfast

2 _____ to bed

3 _____ lunch

4 _____ dinner

5 _____ to school

6 _____ up

7 _____ dressed

8 _____ your teeth

9 _____ in the park

1 Read, look and draw the time.

When do you have breakfast?
At eight o'clock.
At eight o'clock.

What's the time?
It's eight o'clock.
It's eight o'clock.

2 What's the time? Read and circle.

1

It's **one** /
(**two**) o'clock.

2

It's **three** /
four o'clock.

3

It's **seven** /
eight o'clock.

4

It's **eleven** /
twelve o'clock.

3 Write and draw the times for you.

1 I get up at __seven__ o'clock.

2 I have lunch at _____ o'clock.

3 I have dinner at _____ o'clock.

4 I go to bed at _____ o'clock.

1 003 **Can you remember? Listen and write _Brazil_, _Turkey_ or _China_.**

What's the time in Brazil? ...

It's nine o'clock in Brazil
Nine o'clock is cool.
It's nine o'clock in Brazil.
It's time to go to school.

Turkey

What's the time in Turkey? ...

It's three o'clock in Turkey.
My friends are all with me.
It's three o'clock in Turkey
It's time to watch TV.

What's the time in China? ...

It's eight o'clock in China.
The moon is very bright.
It's eight o'clock in China.
It's time to say 'goodnight'.

2 **Read and write the times.**

It's seven o'clock in Brazil.

1 What's the time in Turkey?

It's _____ o'clock.

2 What's the time in China?

It's _____ o'clock.

1 **Look and write.**

goes   goes   has   sleeps   ~~walks~~   watches

Penny **(1)** _walks_ home at seven o'clock.

She **(2)** _____ her dinner at eight.

Then she **(3)** _____ some TV

And **(4)** _____ to bed. It's late!

She's very tired at nine o'clock.

She **(5)** _____ to sleep at ten.

She **(6)** _____ and sleeps and then

It's time to get up again!

2 **Write words to complete the sentences.**

walks   plays   has   has   goes   ~~gets~~

1 Sam _gets_ up at seven o'clock.

2 Sam _____ breakfast at eight o'clock.

3 Sam _____ to school at nine o'clock.

4 Sam _____ in the park at five o'clock.

5 Sam _____ dinner at six o'clock.

6 Sam _____ to bed at ten o'clock.

1 🎧 004 Who says it? Listen and tick ☑.

 1 ☐ ☐

 2 ☐ ☐

 3 ☐ ☐

2 🛡 Look and write the numbers.

1 **Careful, Thunder.**

2 **Sorry, Mum!**

3 **Can you see my keys?**

a ____

b ____

c ____

3 🛡 Who says it? Match.

1 **Careful!**

2 **What's the problem?**

3 **We can play. Hurray!**

a ____

b ____

c ____

1   **Which children are helping? Look and tick ☑.**

2 🎧 005 **Listen and say.**

3 🎧 006 **Listen and circle. Point and say.**

1  king  queen

2  pins  peas

3  chips  cheese

4  fish  feet

Offering to help; phonics focus 15

Read the questions. Listen and write a name or a number.

1 What's the girl's name? <u>Shelley</u>.

2 How old is she? _____.

3 She gets up at _____ o'clock.

4 She has breakfast at _____ o'clock.

5 What's her best friend's name? _____.

 Draw and write about someone in your family.

<u>My dad cooks dinner at</u> _____

<u>seven o'clock.</u> _____

1 **Look and read. Write *yes* or *no*.**

1

Paul gets up at six o'clock.   **no**

2

Paul has got two children.   _____

3

Paul works at a zoo.   _____

4

At one o'clock, Paul has lunch.   _____

5

Paul walks home at 5 o'clock.   _____

6

Paul has dinner with the children.   _____

7

The children go to bed at seven o'clock.   _____

8

In the evening, Paul plays football.   _____

2 **Write two more true sentences about Paul.**

Paul gets up at seven o'clock.

_____

_____

1 **Look and write.**

| shadow | sun | ~~sundial~~ | Roman numbers |

  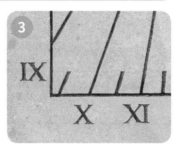 

sundial

2 **Look at the words in Activity 1 and complete the sentences.**

(1) This is a __sundial__. It's old so
(2) it's got _____ _____.
(3) The _____ makes a shadow
on the sundial. To know the time, look
(4) at the _____ and read the
Roman numbers.

3 **Look and draw lines.**

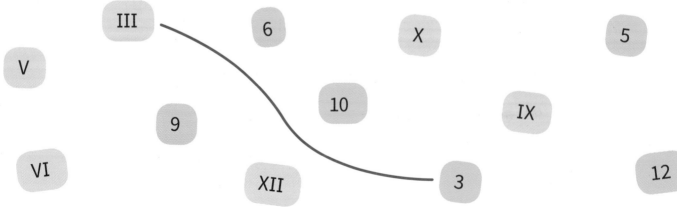

III   6   X   5

V

10

9   IX

VI

XII   3   12

4 Look and write.

Across ➡

a VIII

b IV

c VII

d I

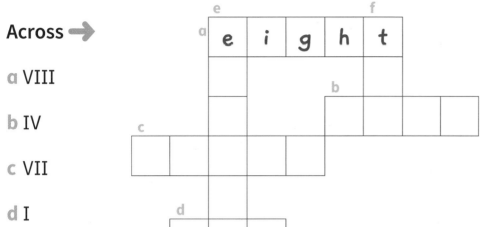

Down ⬇

e XI

f II

5 Look and write the times.

 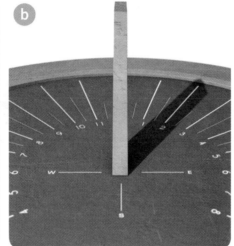 

a _____. b _____. c _____.

6 Look at the clocks in Activity 5. Complete the sentences.

(1) I think clock _____ is very old

(2) and clock _____ is old.

(3) I think clock _____ is new.

Make a diary.

You need

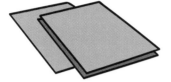

3 sheets of paper

a stapler

pens and pencils

1

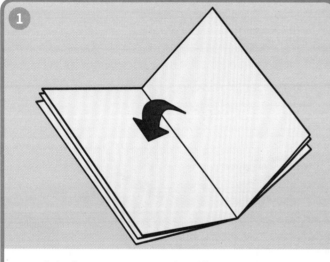

Fold the paper in half.

2

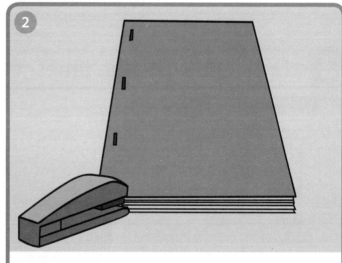

Your teacher staples the paper.

3

Write *My Week* and the days of the week in the diary.

4

Monday

On Monday I play football at 4 o'clock.

Now draw and write in your diary.

1 Write and circle.

1 I can write the names of five daily activities. **Yes / No**

have _____   _____   _____   _____

breakfast _____   _____   _____   _____

2 It's _____ o'clock.

3 Alex _____ at seven o'clock. (get up)

2 Look and write.

BIG QUESTION How do we know the time?

1   s_____

2   s_____

3   R_____
    n_____

4   s_____

3 Read. Then draw and write.

I go to school at 9 o'clock. _____

2 The zoo

1 🛡 **Find the animals and write. Look ➡, ⬇ and ↘.**

zebra _____   _____

p	c	r	o	c	o	d	i	l	e
a	o	r	s	r	p	b	l	a	t
r	o	z	e	b	r	a	e	d	l
r	m	e	i	n	d	n	a	a	v
o	h	h	m	o	n	k	e	y	r
t	v	i	c	t	d	n	o	h	s
e	i	o	p	d	r	f	h	o	n
s	r	g	s	p	s	s	l	w	a
c	l	s	e	m	o	a	u	x	k
p	o	l	a	r	b	e	a	r	e

_____   _____

_____   _____

_____   _____   _____

1 **Read and circle.**

(1) Penny **likes / doesn't like** fish.

(2) She **likes / doesn't like** peas.

Don't give Penny

Any peas, please!

2 **Look and write** *likes* **or** *doesn't like***.**

Tom _likes_____ bananas.

Ben _____ bananas.

Anna _____ apples.

Grace _____ apples.

Jill _____ milk.

Bill _____ milk.

1 008 **Can you remember? Listen and write.**

| bears | crocodiles | hippos | parrots | ~~snakes~~ | tigers |

(1) _Snakes_ like grass
(2) And _____ do too.
They like life
Here in the zoo.

In the zoo, in the zoo …

(3) _____ like trees
(4) And _____ do too.
They like life
Here in the zoo.

In the zoo, in the zoo …

(5) _____ like water
(6) And _____ do too.
They like life
Here in the zoo.

In the zoo, in the zoo …

2 **Draw and write a new verse.**

_____

And _____ do too.

They like life

Here in the zoo.

1 Look, read and tick ☑.

1

a Does Charlie eat bananas for breakfast?

Yes, he does. ☐   No, he doesn't. ☑

b Does Charlie eat bread for breakfast?

Yes, he does. ☐   No, he doesn't. ☐

2

a Does Charlie sleep in a bed?

Yes, he does. ☐   No, he doesn't. ☐

b Does Charlie sleep in a tree?

Yes, he does. ☐   No, he doesn't. ☐

3

a Does Charlie ride a bike to school?

Yes, he does. ☐   No, he doesn't. ☐

b Does Charlie walk to school?

Yes, he does. ☐   No, he doesn't. ☐

2 Look and write *does*, *doesn't* or *like*.

(1) __Does__ Penny (2) _____ crocodiles?

No, she (3) _____ .

(4) _____ Penny (5) _____ polar bears?

(6) Yes, she _____ !

1 🎧 009 Who says it? Listen and tick ☑.

2 Read the story. Then read and tick ☑.

1 Does the  catch the  ?

Yes, he does. ☐
No, he doesn't. ☐

2 Does catch the  ?

Yes, she does. ☐
No, she doesn't. ☐

3 Does  catch the  ?

Yes, she does. ☐
No, she doesn't. ☐

3 Look and write the numbers.

1 Come here, Snake. **2** Let's help him! **3** How does he do that?

a ____

b ____

c ____

1  **Who is helping? Look and tick ☑.**

2 **What's in Kim's bin? What's on Mike's kite? Say and write.**

| fl**y** | ~~s**i**x~~ | sp**i**der | l**i**zard | wh**y** | h**i**ppo | t**i**ger | p**i**n |

Kim's bin

Mike's kite

3 🎧 **010** **Listen, say and check your answers.**

1 🎧 011 Listen and circle.

1 a Does the bear eat carrots?

(Yes, it does.)   No, it doesn't.

b Does the bear come from Canada?

Yes, it does.   No, it doesn't.

2 a Does the hippo come from Africa?

Yes, it does.   No, it doesn't.

b Does the hippo live in the jungle?

Yes, it does.   No, it doesn't.

3 a Does the mouse eat cheese?

Yes, it does.   No, it doesn't.

b And does it live in the jungle?

Yes, it does.   No, it doesn't.

2 Write questions with *like* and answers.

1

Does the parrot like trees _____ ? ✓ Yes, it does .

2

_____ ? ✗ _____ .

3

_____ ? ✗ _____ .

4

_____ ? ✓ _____ .

1 **Read and complete.**

a zebra

I've got four **(1)** <u>legs</u>, two ears, two eyes and lots of
(2) _____ and white stripes. I come from Africa, but now I live in a
(3) _____. I like carrots and **(4)** _____. I don't like bananas.
I drink **(5)** _____. I've got lots of friends here. My best friend is
Charlie. He's a **(6)** _____.

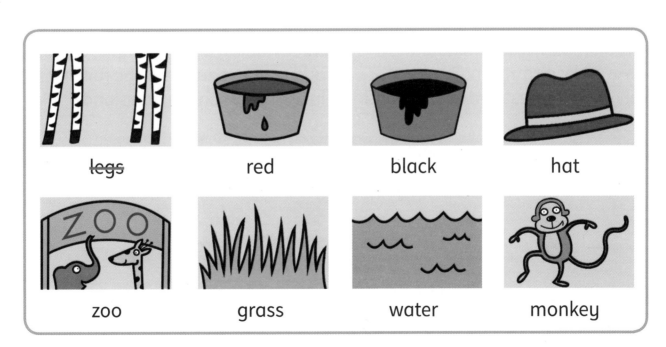

Think and learn

1 **Look and write.**

grassland   ~~ocean~~   polar habitat   rainforest

ocean _____

2 **Read, look and write the animals.**

Where do animals live?

Some animals live in one habitat. For example, zebras live in grassland. Some animals live in two habitats. For example, parrots and tigers can live in the rainforest and in grassland.

And fish can live in the ocean or rainforest. Some animals can live in three habitats! For example, crocodiles and snakes can live in the rainforest, in the ocean and in grassland.

grassland	ocean	rainforest

3 **Look and write numbers.**

1 grassland   **2** rainforest   **3** ocean   **4** polar habitat

4 **Draw two animals in their habitats.**

This is a _____ .

It lives in _____ .

This is a _____ .

It lives in _____ .

1 **Make a zoo.**

You need

paper

wool

tape and glue

pens and pencils

scissors

1

Draw the head and a rectangle for the body.

2

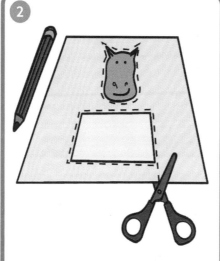

Cut them out.

3

Colour and decorate the head and the body.

4

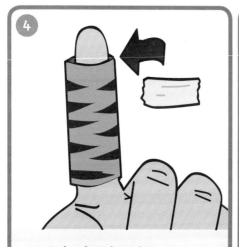

Stick the body around your finger with tape.

5

Glue on the head.

6

Now you can make a zoo!

What do I know? 1 Write and circle.

1 I can write the names of five animals.   **Yes / No**

zebra _____ _____ _____ _____ _____

2 The boys **like / likes** milk.

3 The girl **don't like / doesn't like** apples.

---

2 Look and write.

g_____   o_____   r_____   p_____
                                                   habitat

About me! 3 Read. Then draw and write. _____

My favourite
animal

_____

This is a parrot. _____.

It lives in the rainforest. _____.

3 Where we live

1 Look and draw lines.

shop   hospital   café

cinema   street

train station   bus stop

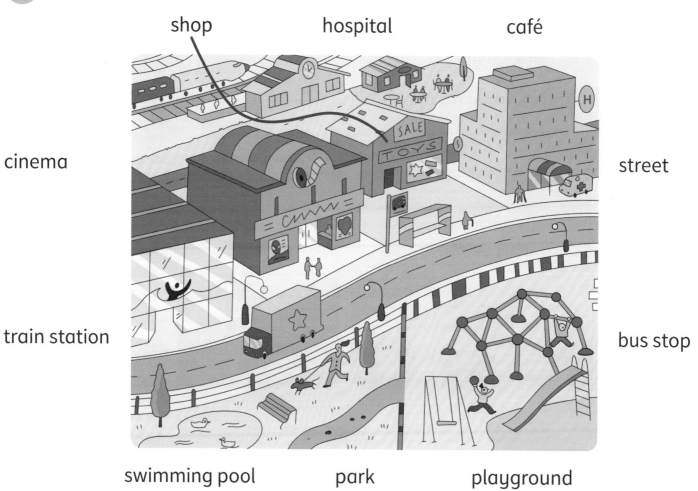

swimming pool   park   playground

2 Match and write the words.

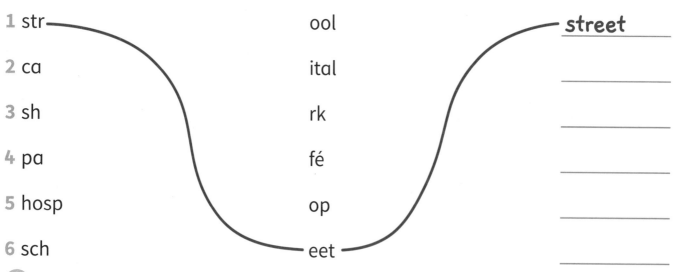

1 str   ool   **street**

2 ca   ital

3 sh   rk

4 pa   fé

5 hosp   op

6 sch   eet

1 Read and circle.

(1) **Has** / **Have** your town got a cinema?

(2) No, it **hasn't** / **haven't**!

(3) **Has** / **Have** your town got a swimming pool?

(4) Yes, it **has** / **have**!

2 Look, read and tick ✓.

1 Has the town got a swimming pool?	Yes, it has. ✓	No, it hasn't. ☐
2 Has the town got a cinema?	Yes, it has. ☐	No, it hasn't. ☐
3 Has the town got a park?	Yes, it has. ☐	No, it hasn't. ☐
4 Has the town got a playground?	Yes, it has. ☐	No, it hasn't. ☐
5 Has the town got a train station?	Yes, it has. ☐	No, it hasn't. ☐

3 Write about your town.

My town has got a park and a shop. It hasn't got a café.

1 012 Can you remember? Listen and write.

✓ = has got   ✗ = hasn't got   ? = doesn't say

1 ?

It's good to have a friend from the town...

Has your town got a playground?
Yes, it has, Sue.
Please tell me how to get there
So I can go with you.

2

It's good to have a friend ...

3

Has your town got a bookshop?
Yes, it has, Jack.
Please tell me how to get there
I can draw it on my map.

4

It's good to have a friend ...

5

Has your town got a café?
No, it hasn't, Jack and Sue.
But let's go to my house.
There's cake and fruit for you.

6

It's good to have a friend ...

2 Write about the town with *has got* and *hasn't got*.

1 The town _____ .

2 The town _____ .

3 The town _____ .

1 **Write the words in the correct order.**

1 is / The fish / the rock / next to
   The fish is next to the rock   .

2 in front of / is / the rock / The fish
   _____.

3 behind / is / The fish / the rock
   _____.

4 the tree / is between / and / the fish / The rock
   _____.

2 **Read and write the words.**

| school | toy shop | cinema | bookshop | ~~café~~ |

1 **café** _____

2 _____

3 _____

4 _____

5 _____

Toy shop

Bookshop

Green Street

In our town, the school is on Green Street. It's in front of the train station. There are a lot of shops on Green Street. Next to the school, there's a toy shop. There's a bookshop between the toy shop and the cinema.

There's a park behind the shops and the cinema. In the park there's a playground and a café – the ice cream there is great!

1 🎧 013 Who says it? Listen and tick ☑.

2 Read and match.

1 What's there on the track?

2 Who runs to stop the train?

3 What does the train driver think?

4 What idea has Flash got?

5 Does the driver stop the train?

6 Who says 'Thanks'?

a The girl is fast.

b The driver.

c A big tree.

d Yes, he does.

e Flash.

f She writes 'STOP'.

3 Order the sentences. Write numbers.

☐ The driver doesn't understand.

8 The driver says 'Thanks'.

4 Flash says 'Stop the train!'

☐ Flash runs down the hill.

☐ The driver stops the train.

☐ They see a tree on the train track.

☐ Flash writes 'STOP'.

1 The Super Friends are on a hill.

1 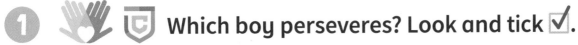 Which boy perseveres? Look and tick ☑.

Oh no!

Oh no!

2 Look and write.

| t̶r̶ | br | tr | gr | cr | dr | dr | br |

t r ee

have ___eakfast

get ___essed

___ush your teeth

___ocodile

___andmother

___ain ___iver

3 🎧 014 Listen, say and check your answers.

1 🎧 015 Listen and write S (Sarah), O (Oscar) or C (Cheryl).

1 Where?

  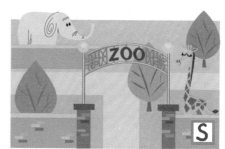

2 With?

3 When?

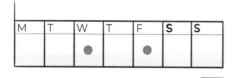

4 What?

2 🛡 Read and write.

I go to my favourite shop with my mum on Saturdays. I read a book there every week!

Grace's favourite place is the _____ .

1 Look at the pictures and the letters. Write the words.

p a r k   r k a p

_ _ _ _ _   h s p s o

_ _ _ _ _ _   a m i n c e

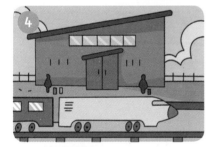

_ _ _ _ _ _   t t n i o a s

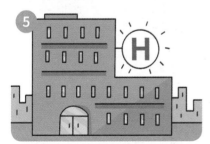

_ _ _ _ _ _ _   l p i a h s o t

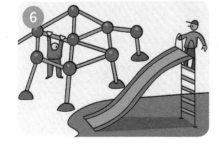

_ _ _ _ _ _ _ _ _   g l d n y a u o r p

1 Look and write.

| car park | ~~market~~ | monument | sports centre | museum |

market _____ _____ _____ _____

2 Where can you find each object? Look and draw lines.

car park

market

sports centre

museum

3 Look and write the letters and numbers.

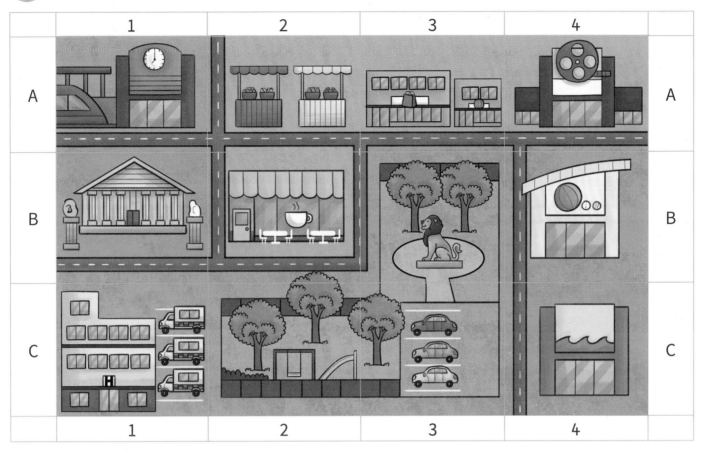

1 swimming pool **4C**

2 sports centre _____

3 train station _____

4 monument _____

5 shops _____

6 car park _____

4 Look at Activity 3. Write words to complete the puzzle.

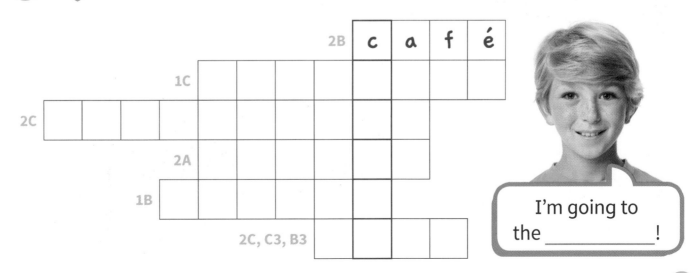

2B | c | a | f | é

I'm going to the _____!

1 Make a box town.

You need

 boxes and tubes

 tape and glue

 coloured paper

 tissue

 scissors

 pens and pencils

1
Stick coloured paper on the boxes and tubes.

2
Stick on doors and windows.

3
Add chimneys and use tissue to make smoke.

4
Decorate your building.

5
Now you can make a box town.

1 Write and circle.

1 I can write the names of five places in a town.   **Yes** / **No**

__playground__   _____   _____   _____   _____

2 Has the street got a café?
Yes, it has. / **No, it hasn't.**

3 The bus stop is **in front of** / **next to** the cinema.

---

2 Look, read and write.

BIG QUESTION How can we find places?

1 What's in 1A?   a _____

2 What's in 2B?   a _____

3 Where's the monument?   It's in _____ .

---

3 Read. Then draw and write.   _____

My favourite place

I love the café in my town.

I eat ice cream there.

_____

_____

4 The market

1 Do the crossword.

1 Read and circle.

(1) **Would you** / **Do you** like a pizza, Penny?

Yes, please.

(2) Would you like **a** / **some** bread?

Yes, please.

Would you like some ice cream?

(3) **Yes, please.** / **No, thank you.** I think I need my bed.

2 Write *a*, *an* or *some*.

1   Would you like **a**_____ tomato?   Yes, please.

2   Would you like _____ lemon?   No, thank you.

3   Would you like _____ egg?   Yes, please.

4   Would you like _____ grapes?   No, thank you.

5   Would you like _____ orange?   Yes, please.

3 Write the words in the correct order.

1 you / like / an / Would / orange

__Would you like an orange__ ?

Yes, please.

2 a / like / you / mango / Would

_____ ?

Yes, please.

3 like / bread / Would / you / some

_____ ?

No, thank you.

4 some / like / you / fish / Would

_____ ?

No, thank you.

1 🎧 **016** 🛡 **Can you remember? Listen and write.**

(1) Would you like an 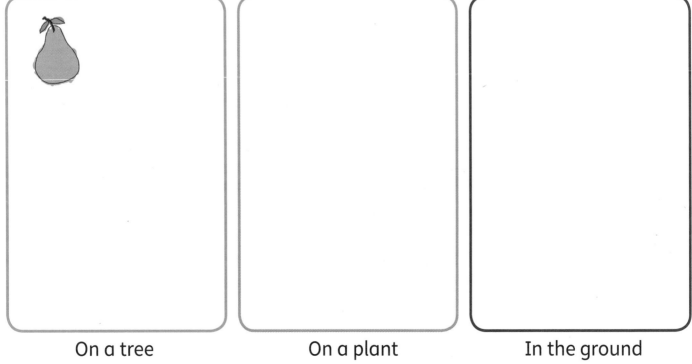 _____?

(2) Would you like a _____?

There's lots of fruit and vegetables

Lots for us to share.

Super fruits and vegetables.

Pick them from the tree

(3) Lemons, pears and _____, too.

Pick one for you

And one for me.

Super fruits and vegetables

Grow them in the ground

(4) Carrots, _____,

(5) _____, too

There's good food all around.

2 🛡 **Draw the food from Activity 1. Where does it grow?**

On a tree	On a plant	In the ground

1 **Look, read and tick ☑.**

1 Are there any grapes?   Yes, there are. ☑   No, there aren't. ☐

2 Are there any lemons?   Yes, there are. ☐   No, there aren't. ☐

3 Are there any watermelons? Yes, there are. ☐   No, there aren't. ☐

4 Is there any chicken?   Yes, there is. ☐   No, there isn't. ☐

5 Are there any eggs?   Yes, there are. ☐   No, there aren't. ☐

2 **Look and circle.**

1 (Is) / **Are** there any cheese in the house?

a No, there **isn't** / **aren't** any.

b Yes, there **is** / **are**.

2 **Is** / **Are** there any grapes in the house?

a No, there **isn't** / **aren't** any.

b Yes, there **is** / **are**.

3 **Write about your school bag.**

There is an apple in my bag. There isn't a mango.

1 🎧 **017** **Who says it? Listen and tick ☑.**

2 **Order the sentences. Write numbers.**

☐ Misty has got an idea.

☐ The man gives the bag of apples to the children.

1 Flash gives her friends some apples.

☐ Misty sees two boxes of apples.

☐ The children show everyone the apples!

5 The children ask for eight apples.

☐ Each friend has got one bad apple.

☐ The man puts four good apples and four bad apples in a bag.

3 🛡 **Look and write the numbers.**

1 We know what we can do!

2 What can we do?

3 Well done!

1  Who is cheating? Look and tick ☑.

1

 ☐

2

 ☐

2 🎧 018 Listen and follow. Say the number.

3 🎧 019 Listen again and say.

1 🎧 020 **What do they like? Listen and tick ☑.**

	Sandra	John	Mum	Dad
chicken	✓	✓	✓	✓
potatoes				
beans				
tomatoes				
orange juice				
water				

2 🛡 **Write about your family.**

Hi, I'm Mei. I live in Beijing. In our family, we often
eat pizza. I like orange juice but my sister doesn't.
She likes milk.

1 Look, read and tick ☑ or cross ☒.

1 This is a pear. ☑

2 This is an orange. ☐

3 This is a cake. ☐

4 This is a bean. ☐

5 This is an egg. ☐

6 This is a mango. ☐

7 This is some bread. ☐

WEIGHTS

1 How many grams do they weigh? Look and write.

a four mangoes ___800g___

b five eggs _____

c four potatoes _____

d three tomatoes _____

e ten grapes _____

f two kiwis _____

2 Order the weights. Label the chart.

 **a**
75g

 **b**
100g

 **c**
5g

 **d**
200g

 **e**
50g

 **f**
150g

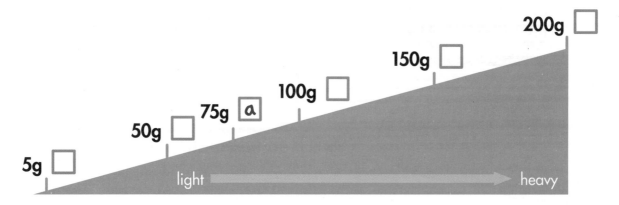

200g ☐

150g ☐

100g ☐

75g [a]

50g ☐

5g ☐

light ➡ heavy

③ Do the food sums.

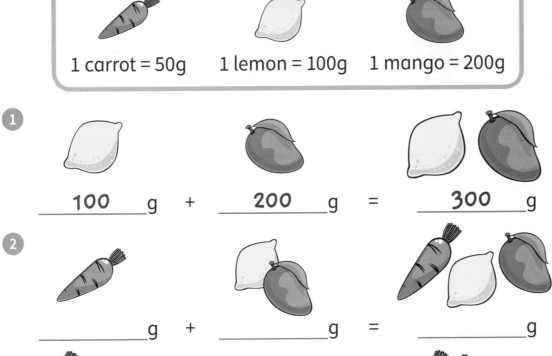

1 carrot = 50g   1 lemon = 100g   1 mango = 200g

1

_____**100**_____ g   +   _____**200**_____ g   =   _____**300**_____ g

2

_____ g   +   _____ g   =   _____ g

3

      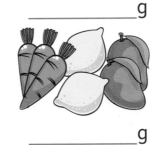

_____ g   +   _____ g   =   _____ g

4

_____ g   +   _____ g   =   _____ g

④ Look, read and answer _yes_ or _no_.

500g of watermelon weighs the same as 500g of grapes.

Is it true?

_____

1 **Make a potato person.**

You need

 scissors   clean potatoes   wool   toothpicks   glue   paper   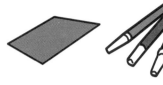 pens

1

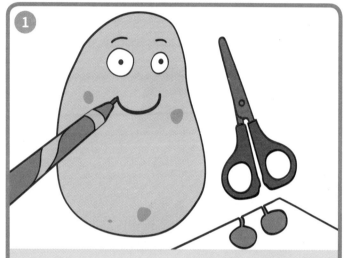

Give your potato a face with pens, glue and paper.

2

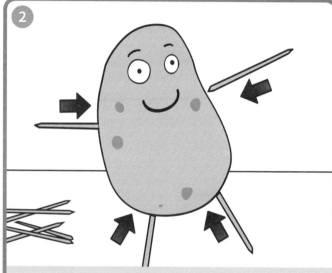

Use toothpicks for arms and legs.

3

Use wool for hair.

4

Use paper for the clothes.
Now you have a potato person!

1 Write and circle.

1 I can write the names of five foods.   **Yes / No**

bread _____   _____   _____   _____   _____

2 Is there any fruit?

Yes, there is. / No, there isn't.

3 Are there any vegetables?

Yes, there are. / No, there aren't.

  2 Order the sentences. Write numbers.

BIG QUESTION How can we buy food?

a Go to a shop, market or supermarket. ☐

b Make a shopping list. **1**

c Say 'thank you' to the shopkeeper. ☐

d Say 'ten carrots, please' or '500g of carrots'. ☐

  3 Read. Then draw and write. _____

My favourite fruit

I love mangoes! I eat them in a fruit salad.

1 **Read and colour.**

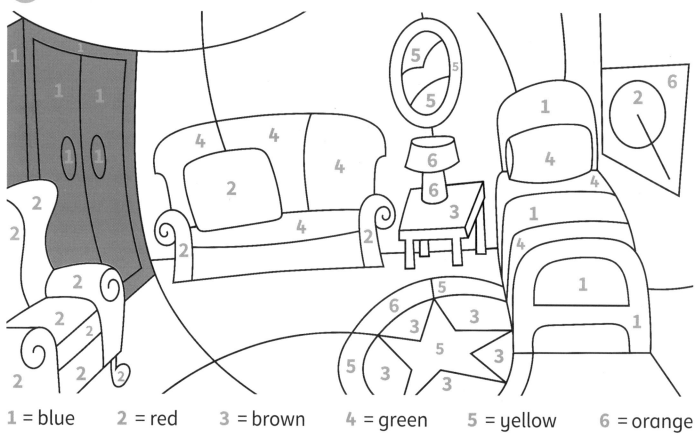

1 = blue   2 = red   3 = brown   4 = green   5 = yellow   6 = orange

2 **Look at Activity 1. Write the words.**

> bed   sofa   lamp   rug   armchair
> mirror   ~~wardrobe~~   table   poster

1 The **wardrobe** is blue.

2 The _____ is orange.

3 The _____ is brown.

4 The _____ is red.

5 The _____ is yellow.

6 The _____ is blue and green.

7 The _____ is red and orange.

8 The _____ is red and green.

9 The _____ is brown, yellow and orange.

1 Look and draw lines.

1 I like these armchairs.

2 This bed is fun!

3 I like those rugs.

4 That wardrobe is nice.

2 Look, read and circle.

These / (Those) chairs are great.

I like **this / that** table.

This / That mirror is lovely.

I like **these / those** armchairs.

3 Write the words in the correct order.

1 this / I / wardrobe / like

   I like this wardrobe   .

2 chair / like / I / that

   _____ .

3 I / posters / these / like

   _____ .

4 lovely / those / I / lamps / like

   _____ .

1 🎧 **021** 🛡 **Can you remember? Listen and circle.**

(1) Give me a piece of **food** / (**wood**),

Let's see what I can do.

(2) Let's **cut** / **cook** and paint and make

Some furniture for you.

Take that piece of wood,

(3) **Chop** / **Cut** it and paint it red.

Put it all together now.

(4) Wow! I like this **bread** / **bed**.

Take that piece of wood,

(5) Cut it and **paint some squares** / **eat some pears**.

Put it all together now.

(6) Wow! I like these **stairs** / **chairs**.

2 🛡 **Draw and write a new verse.**

Take that piece of _____

_____ it and _____

Put it all together now.

Wow! _____ .

1 **Look and circle.**

(1) Whose shoes are (these)/ **this**? (3) Whose hat is **these** / **this**?

(2) **It's** / **They're** Penny's shoes. (4) **It's** / **They're** Penny's hat.

2 **Follow the lines and write.**

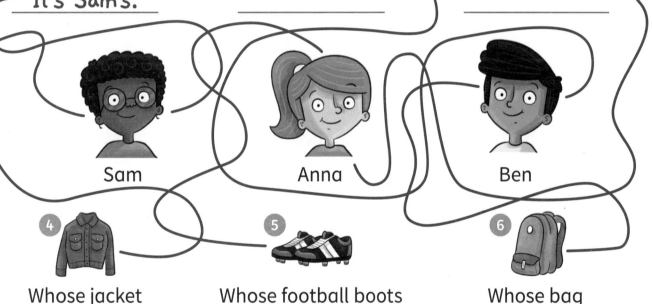

1 Whose baseball cap is this?
It's Sam's. _____

2 Whose socks are these?
_____

3 Whose jumper is this?
_____

Sam

Anna

Ben

4 Whose jacket is this?
_____

5 Whose football boots are these?
_____

6 Whose bag is this?
_____

3 **Look and match.**

1  Whose boots are these?   ☐ It's my pen.

2 Whose pen is this?   ☐ No, it's not Jane's. It's mine.

3  Whose bike is this? Is it Jane's?   ☐ 1 They're Jane's boots.

1 🎧 **022** **Who says it? Listen and tick ☑.**

2 **Read and circle.**

1 Sorry Whisper, not now. She's tidying up (her room)/ the kitchen.

2 Just a minute. Let me **see** / **check** first.

3 I don't like tidying up. Ah, I've got **a problem** / **an idea**!

4 **Sorry** / **Thank you**, Mum. No park for me today.

3 🛡 **Look and write the numbers.**

1   **Whose room is tidy? Look and tick ☑.**

2 **Say and write the words under *look* or *school*.**

~~book~~   p**oo**l   z**oo**   g**oo**d   f**oo**d   f**oo**tball

look

book

_____

_____

school

_____

_____

_____

3 **023** **Listen, say and check your answers.**

1 🎧 024 **Listen and draw lines.**

Sam   Dan   Alice   Tom

Lucy   Max   Grace

1 **Read and write the words.**

> are   is   sofas   sunny
> ~~swimming~~   snow

A holiday in ice and snow!

Many people go to hot countries for their holidays. They like
(1) _swimming_ in the sea and they love the (2) _____ weather.
Other people go to cold countries because they like the (3) _____.
The Ice Hotel is a great place for these people. It is in Canada.

Would you like a holiday in the Ice Hotel? Everything is ice!
There (4) _____ big, beautiful ice lamps. There (5) _____
an ice restaurant and there are 80 ice
bedrooms. In the bedrooms, there are ice
tables, ice armchairs, ice (6) _____ and,
of course, ice beds too. But don't worry – you
get two very warm sleeping bags for the night!

2 **Write about your bedroom.**

In my bedroom, there is a big bed, a wardrobe and there
are two small bookcases. The bed is blue and the wardrobe
is white. The bookcases are brown.

Materials

1 **Look and write.**

fabric   glass   metal   plastic   ~~wood~~

wood _____ _____ _____ _____

2 **Read and draw lines.**

1 It's made of glass and wood.

2 It's made of metal and plastic. I use it every day!

3 It's made of fabric. It's got lots of different colours.

4 It's lovely – it's made of wood and fabric.

5 It's made of wood. I want to paint it!

3 What's in your house? Look, write and tick ✓.

	fabric	glass	metal	plastic	wood
bed	✓				✓

4 Look at Activity 3. Write sentences.

1 My bed is made of fabric and wood .

2 _____ .

3 _____ .

4 _____ .

5 Choose, write and draw.

fabric   glass   metal   ~~plastic~~   wood

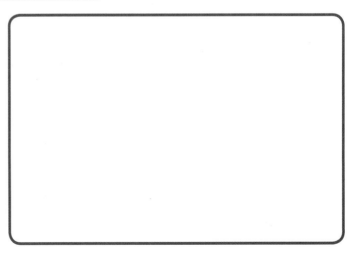

They're made of **plastic** .

They're made of _____ .

1 **Make a picture from paper and plastic.**

You need

| a sheet of card | different kinds of paper and plastic | scissors | glue |

Stick the pieces of paper and plastic on the card to make your picture.

1 Write and circle.

1 I can write the names of five kinds of furniture.   **Yes / No**

armchair _____ _____ _____ _____

2 Whose baseball cap is **this / these**?
It's / They're Grace's.

3 Whose trainers are **this / these**?
It's / They're Dan's.

Grace   Dan

2 Look, read and tick ✓ or cross ✗.

BIG QUESTION **What does furniture look like?**

  It's made of paper. ☐

 It's made of plastic. ☐

 It's made of wood. ☐

3 Read. Then draw and write. _____

My favourite thing in my room	

My lamp is red and yellow. _____

It's made of metal and fabric. _____

6 People

1 Use the letters to make *face* words.

r e e a h
s n c t s

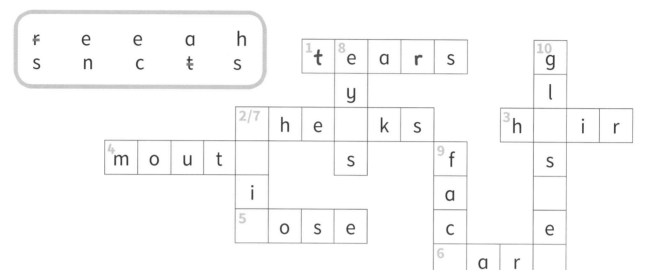

2 Write the words.

1

face

4   5   6   7

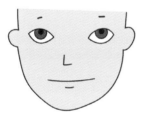

1 Read and circle.

1

Jill is **sad** / **tired** / (**excited**).

2

Kim is **sad** / **scared** / **happy**.

3

Bill is **tired** / **angry** / **happy**.

4

Sue is **sad** / **happy** / **angry**.

5

Ben is **tired** / **angry** / **sad**.

6

Nick is **angry** / **excited** / **tired**.

2 Look and write.

~~angry~~	excited	happy	tired

(1) Are you __angry__ ?   Are you happy?

No, I'm not angry.   **(3)** Yes, I'm _____

(2) I'm not _____ .   **(4)** and _____ .

1 025  **Can you remember? Listen and write.**

face	happy	sad	scared	tired

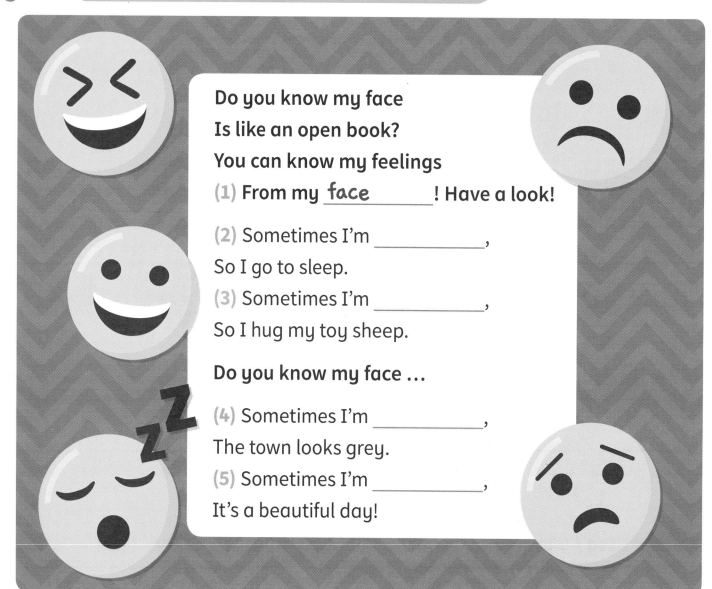

Do you know my face
Is like an open book?
You can know my feelings
(1) From my ___face___ ! Have a look!

(2) Sometimes I'm _____ ,
So I go to sleep.
(3) Sometimes I'm _____ ,
So I hug my toy sheep.

Do you know my face …

(4) Sometimes I'm _____ ,
The town looks grey.
(5) Sometimes I'm _____ ,
It's a beautiful day!

2 **Write a new verse.**

Sometimes I'm _____ ,
_____ .
Sometimes I'm _____ ,
_____ .

happy

excited

sad

scared

angry

tired

6

1 Number the months.

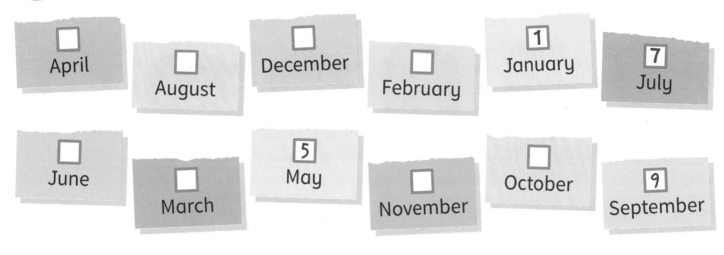

April	☐
August	☐
December	☐
February	☐
January	1
July	7
June	☐
March	☐
May	5
November	☐
October	☐
September	9

2 Look and match.

1 My birthday is in April.

2 Their birthdays are in November.

3 Our birthdays are in March.

4 Its birthday is in May.

 a ☐

 b 1

 c ☐

 d ☐

3 Look and write.

(1) O **u** **r** birthdays aren't in May.

They aren't in September.

(2) O __ __ birthdays are in November!

(3) T __ __ __ __ birthdays aren't in May.

They aren't in September.

(4) T __ __ __ __ birthdays are in December!

The months, *our*, *their* 73

1 🎧 **026** **Who says it? Listen and tick ✓.**

 1 □ □

 2 □ □

 3 □ □

2 **Look and match.**

1 three-legged race

2 tug of war

3 *Pin the tail on the donkey*

a

b

c

3 **Look and write the numbers.**

1 That's not fair!

2 Pull, pull, pull, you can win this tug of war!

3 Oh dear!

a ___

b ___

c ___

1   Who is being a good loser? Look and tick ☑.

2 Read and colour the train.

> train = **red**   sad = **blue**

train

sad

thanks

play

face

cap

race

lamp

3 🎧 **027** Listen, say and check your picture.

1 🎧 028 Listen and tick ✓.

1 Which is Emma's best friend?

a  ✓

b  ☐

c  ☐

2 Which is Emma's brother?

a  ☐

b  ☐

c  ☐

3 Which is Jenny?

a  ☐

b  ☐

c  ☐

4 Which is Emma's dad?

a  ☐

b  ☐

c  ☐

5 Which is Ben?

a  ☐

b  ☐

c  ☐

1 **Read and write the words.**

> 38   afternoon   birthday   eleven   football
> May   park   sister   ~~Sunday~~

1

Dear Sam,

Please come to my birthday party on **(1)** _Sunday_ .
It starts at two o'clock. The party is next to the lake
in the **(2)** _____ . Can you bring your new
(3) _____ ? We can play a big game with everyone.

See you there!

Matt

2 PARTY

Dear Finn,

Please come to my
(1) _____ party on
Saturday. It's in the village
hall. You can bring your
(2) _____ . She can play
with my little brother. The
party starts at three o'clock in
the **(3)** _____ .

See you then!

Emily

3 BIRTHDAY

Dear Lily,

Please come to my birthday
party on Saturday 6th
(1) _____ . The party is
in our garden, at my house –
(2) _____ Franklin Road.
It starts at **(3)** _____
o'clock in the morning.

Can you come?

Isabel

Think and learn

Portraits

1 **Look and write.**

| drawing | painting | ~~paper collage~~ | photo |

paper collage _____   _____   _____

2 🛡 **Read and draw lines.**

b

1 I'm taking a picture of an angry boy. The angry boy is me!

a

2 I'm drawing with my friends! We love trees and animals.

3 I'm making a paper collage. It's of my brother and my sister.

d

c

4 I've got a self-portrait. That's a picture of myself! It's a painting.

3 **Look, read and match.**

① 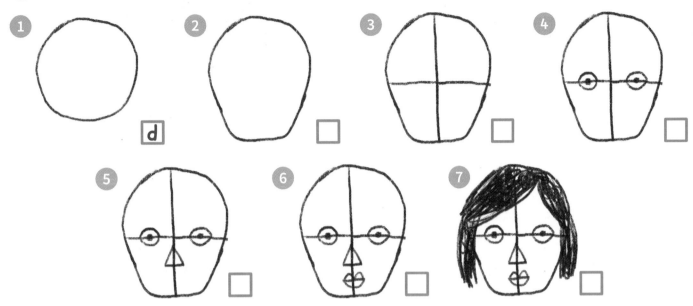 **d**

② ☐

③ ☐

④ ☐

⑤ ☐

⑥ ☐

⑦ ☐

a Draw eyes on the line across the middle.

b Add some hair!

c Draw a nose between the eyes and the chin.

d Start with a circle.

e Draw one line down the middle. Then draw one line across the middle.

f Add a chin.

g Draw a mouth in the middle between the nose and the chin.

4   **Look at Activity 3. Draw a self-portrait.**

This is my self-portrait.

I have got _____

_____

_____ .

1 Make an emoji birthday card.

You need

a sheet of card   scissors   pens

1

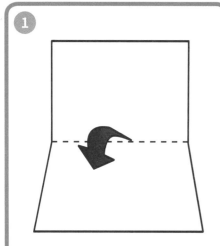

Fold the card in half.

2

Draw an emoji.

3

Colour your emoji.

4

Cut out your emoji. Don't cut on the fold!

5

Happy Birthday Mum

Write on your card.

6

It's an emoji birthday card.

1 Write and circle.

1 I can write the names of five parts of the face.   **Yes / No**

___eyes___   _____   _____   _____   _____

2 Is he sad? **Yes, he is. / No, he isn't.**

3 **His / Their** birthdays are in August.

BIG QUESTION **How are faces different?**

2 🛡 Look and circle.

1 Faces can be happy or (sad)/ **drawings**.

2 They can have green eyes or **short / brown** eyes.

3 They can have long or **sad / short** hair.

4 They can be in photos, paper collages, paintings or **drawings / brown**.

3 🛡 Read. Then draw and write.

Today, I feel ___excited___

because ___it's my birthday.___

Today, I feel _____

because _____

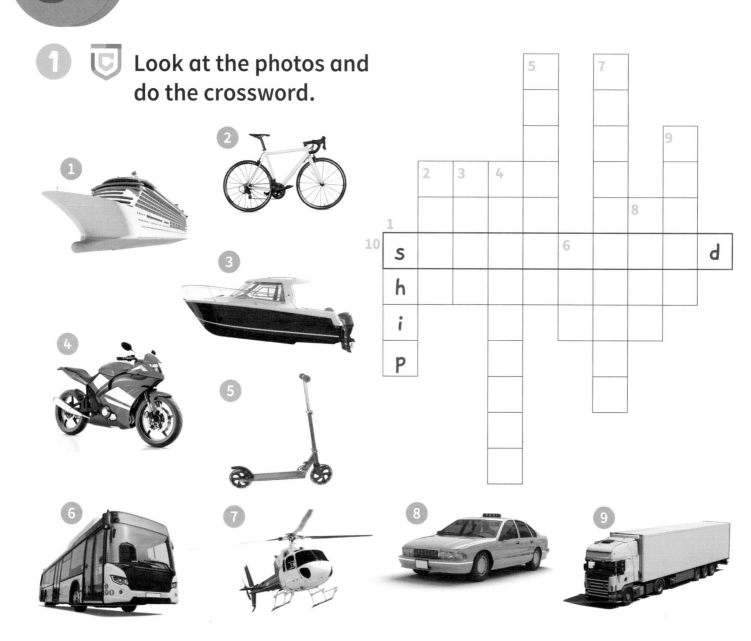

7 Off we go!

1 Look at the photos and do the crossword.

2 Look at Activity 1.
Draw number 10.

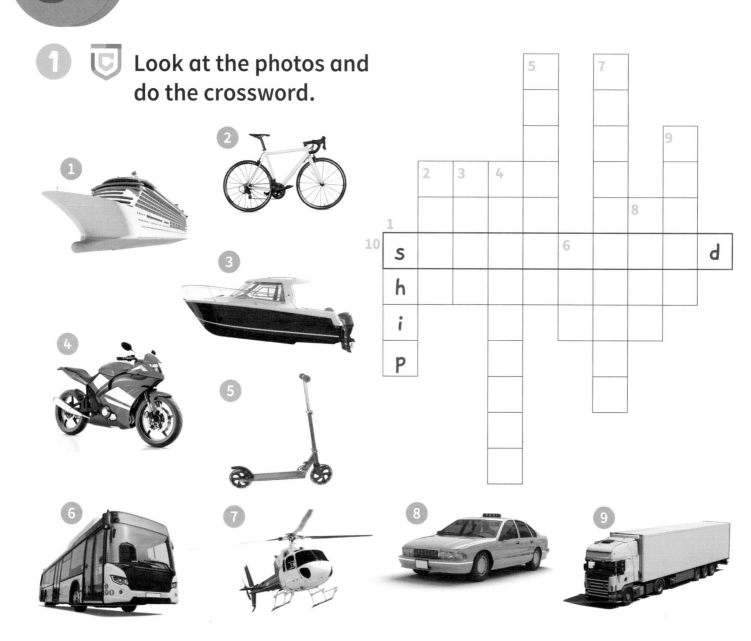

1 Read and circle.

(1) I'd like **go** / **to go** to Brazil by plane!

(2) **I'd** / **I** like to go to Brazil.

(3) I'd like **go** / **to go** to Spain by bus!

(4) **I'd** / **I** like to go to Spain!

2 Read, look and match.

1 I'd like to fly a helicopter.

2 I'd like to drive a lorry.

3 I'd like to sail a boat.

a b c

☐ ☐ ☐

3 Write the words in the correct order.

1 to / I'd / ride / a / motorbike / like
  I'd like to ride a motorbike _____.

2 like / sail / a / ship / I'd / to
  _____.

3 I'd / to / a / bus / like / drive
  _____.

4 fly / like / I'd / to / a / plane
  _____.

1 🎧 029 🛡 Can you remember? Listen and write.

| car | ~~far~~ | close | plane | skateboard | rocket |

I'd like to go to Africa.

(1) I think it's very **far** _____.

(2) I'd like to go there on a _____.

It's too far for a car.

For a car.

I'd like to go to my friend's house

It's not so very far.

(3) I'd like to go on my _____.

(4) It's too _____ for a car.

For a car.

I'd like to go to outer space.

I know it's very far.

(5) I'd like to take a _____ there.

(6) It's too far for a _____.

For a car.

2 🛡 Write a new verse.

I'd like to go to _____.

I'd like to _____.

_____.

It's _____.

1 Complete the questions.

(1) _____ a bus?   (you / drive)

No, I'm not!

(2) What _____?   (you / do)

I'm driving a taxi! Toot toot!

2 Look and draw lines.

1 He's waiting for a bus.

2 She's riding a scooter.

3 He's riding a motorbike.

4 She's skateboarding.

5 He's sailing a boat.

6 She's riding a bike.

3 Read and match.

1 What are you doing?

2 Are you watching TV?

3 Are you eating chocolate?

4 Is he doing his homework?

5 What is she doing?

6 Is she sleeping?

a ☐ No, I'm not. I'm watching a DVD.

b ☐ Yes, he is.

c ☐ She's having a shower.

d ☐1 I'm looking for my bag.

e ☐ No, she isn't.

f ☐ Yes, I am. Would you like some?

1 🎧 **030** **Who says it? Listen and tick** ✓.

2 **Read and circle. Then read the story and check.**

1 The children are feeling **sad** / (**excited**).

2 The children want to go to the **beach** / **airport**.

3 They are on a **plane** / **bus**.

4 First, there are **ships** / **sheep** on the road.

5 Then there is a problem with the **tyre** / **window**.

6 Then, they arrive at the **beach** / **airport**.

3 **Look and write the numbers.**

1 Now it's my turn to help you!

2 No problem.

3 I think I can help.

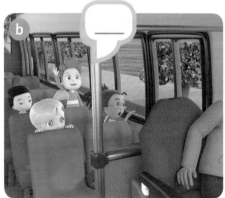

1  Who is being generous? Look and tick ☑.

2 Write the letters.

oe   ou   ~~wo~~   ue   oo   ui

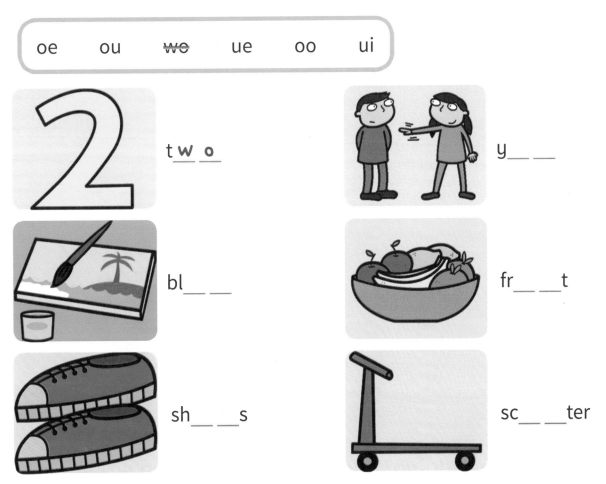

t **w** **o**

y___ ___

bl___ ___

fr___ ___t

sh___ ___s

sc___ ___ter

3 🎧 031 Listen, say and check your answers.

1 🎧 032 **Listen and colour.**

2 **What are they doing? Look at the picture and write.**

1 The boy is _____ . **2** The girl is _____ .

1 How does Rick travel? Read, look and draw lines.

Hi, my name's Rick. I like visiting my friends and family. My cousin Luke lives on a farm with lots of animals. When we visit him, we go by car.

When we visit Grandma Sue, we go by train. She lives in a big city. I love that because I love trains.

When we visit Grandma Pat, we go by plane. She lives in Spain, by the sea.

My best friend is called Tony. When I go to his house, I ride my bike. He lives on a boat near my house.

1 Luke   2 Sue   3 Pat   4 Tony

a   b   c   d

2 Read again. Who lives there? Write the names.

1 Pat   2 _____   3 _____   4 _____

Think and learn

Transport

1 Where do they go? Write numbers.

① in the air

② on land

③ on water

a

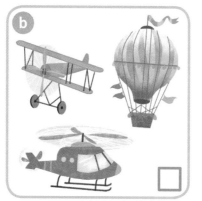
b

c

2 Where are the photos from? Look and write.

in the air   on land   on water

1

2

3

on water

4

5

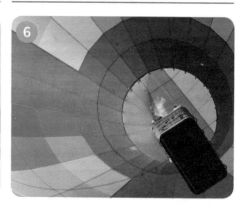
6

3 **What do they need? Write a letter.**

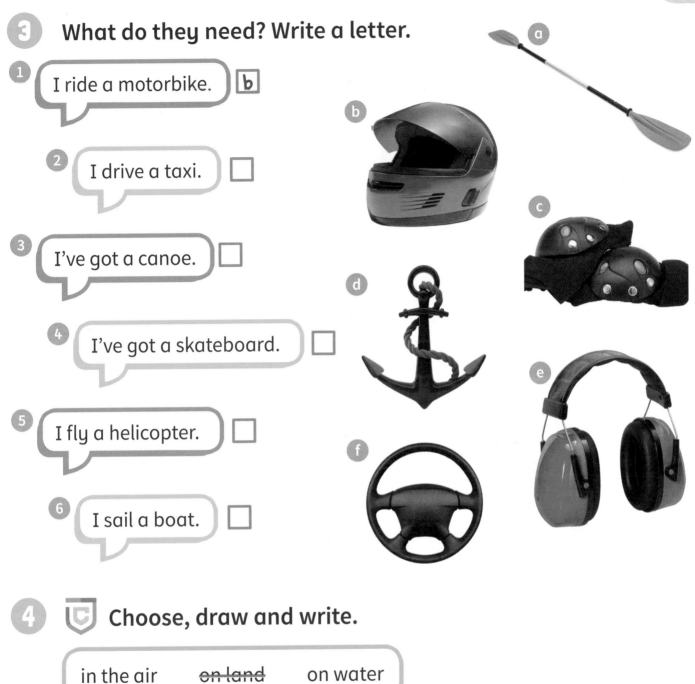

1 I ride a motorbike. **b**

2 I drive a taxi. ☐

3 I've got a canoe. ☐

4 I've got a skateboard. ☐

5 I fly a helicopter. ☐

6 I sail a boat. ☐

4 **Choose, draw and write.**

in the air   ~~on land~~   on water

They go on land.

car   motorbike   lorry

1 Make a speed boat.

You need

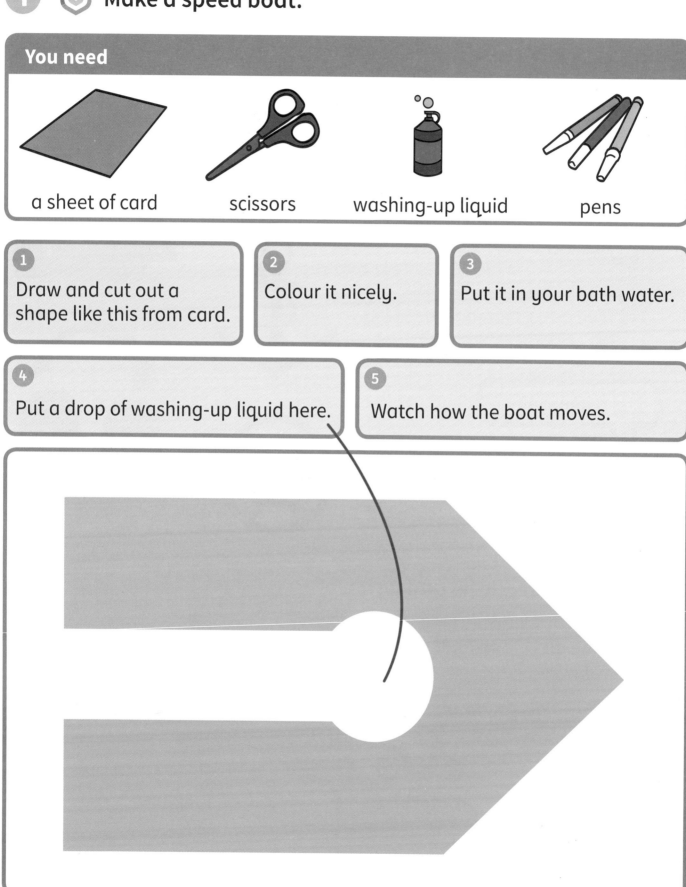

a sheet of card · scissors · washing-up liquid · pens

1 Draw and cut out a shape like this from card.

2 Colour it nicely.

3 Put it in your bath water.

4 Put a drop of washing-up liquid here.

5 Watch how the boat moves.

 1 **Write and circle.**

1 I can write five modes of transport. **Yes / No**

__helicopter__ _____ _____ _____ _____

2 I'd like **drive / to drive** a train.

3 Is she riding a bike?
Yes, she is. /
No, she isn't.

---

2 **Look and write.**

BIG QUESTION **Where can transport go?**

in the air   on water   on land

_____   _____   _____

---

3 **Read. Then draw and write.**

__I'd like to sail a ship.__ _____

1 **Look and write.**

swimming	baseball	football	basketball	tennis
volleyball	~~badminton~~	athletics	basketball	table tennis	hockey

1 __badminton__   2 _____   3 _____

4 _____   5 _____   6 _____

7 _____   8 _____   9 _____

10 _____

1 Write -ing forms of the words.

~~fly~~   listen   make   paint   play   read   ride   watch

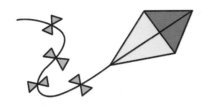

1 **flying** a kite

2 _____ pictures

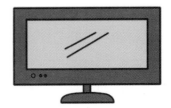

3 _____ TV

4 _____ a sandcastle

5 _____ to music

6 _____ horses

7 _____ a book

8 _____ a guitar

2 Read and write.

(1) Playing football's **fun** _____. (n u f)

Dancing's great.

(2) Flying a kite's _____. (d t u f i c l i f)

(3) But swimming's _____! (y e s a)

3 Write sentences for you.

1 _____ is great!

2 _____ is boring.

1 **033**  **Can you remember? Listen and match the items with each verse.**

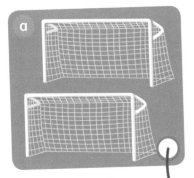

(1) __Playing__ sport is easy.

It's all I want to do.

I'd like to play with you.

(2) Playing sport is great _____

It's all I want to do.

I'd like to play with you.

Give me a pitch,

Give me some friends,

(3) Give me a _____ to play.

Now we need two goals.

Let's play football all day.

Give me a court,

(4) Give me some _____,

Give me a ball to play.

Now we need a net.

(5) Let's _____ volleyball all day.

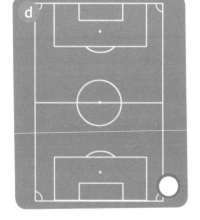

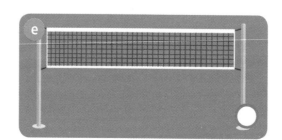

2 **Look at Activity 1. Write the words.**

| ball | fun | friends | play | ~~playing~~ |

1 Read and circle.

(1) What sport do you like **do** / **doing**?

(2) I like **play** / **playing** football.

So do I.

(3) I like **play** / **playing** tennis.

Me too!

(4) I like **swim** / **swimming**.

I don't. No, no, no!

2 Write the words.

What sport do you like doing?

(2) Me too! Do you like _____ _____?

(3) I don't. I like _____ _____.

Yes, I do.

(5) Do you like _____ _____?

(1) I like _playing hockey_ _____.

Yes, I do.

(4) So do I. Do you like _____ _____?

(6) No, I don't. I like _____ _____.

1 🎧 034 Who says it? Listen and tick ✓.

2 Read and tick ✓ the boxes.

1 Flash wants to play football.   yes ✓   no ☐

2 At first, the boy wants Flash in his team.   yes ☐   no ☐

3 Misty wants to join the table tennis club.   yes ☐   no ☐

4 Misty scores a goal.   yes ☐   no ☐

5 The green team wins the football game.   yes ☐   no ☐

6 At the end, the boy wants Flash in his team.   yes ☐   no ☐

3 Look and write the numbers.

1 Ha, ha. It's going to be very easy.

2 Well done, Flash!

3 Join our team!

1   **Who is including people? Look and tick ☑.**

2 **Read and colour the sock.**

hockey = **orange**   hippo = yellow

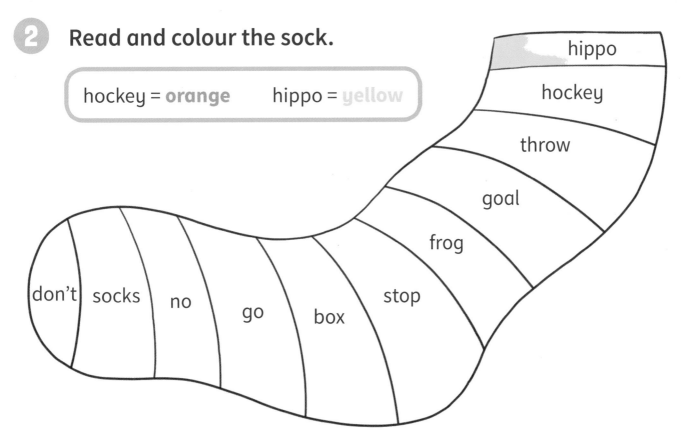

3 🎧 035 **Listen, say and check your picture.**

1 Look and read. Write *yes* or *no*.

1 Two boys are playing badminton.   yes

2 Some boys are playing volleyball.   _____

3 There's a woman behind the table tennis table.   _____

4 A woman is taking a photo.   _____

5 The man has got a dog.   _____

6 The tennis players are wearing baseball caps.   _____

1 🎧 **036** **Listen and complete. Write one word in each space.**

1 What club does the boy want to join?
<u>Badminton</u>.

2 When is the club?
Mondays and _____.

3 Where is the club?
In the school _____ hall.

4 Who is the club for?
_____.

2 **Look and write sentences.**

1 <u>One boy is playing baseball.</u>   3 _____

2 _____   4 _____

Sports equipment

1 **Look and write.**

bat   board   goggles   ~~helmet~~   net   racket

helmet   _____   _____   _____   _____   _____

2 **Read, think and write.**

tennis   baseball   badminton   ~~football~~   volleyball

	racket	bat	net	ball
1 football				✓
2 _____	✓		✓	
3 _____		✓		✓
4 _____	✓		✓	✓
5 _____			✓	✓

3 Look and write *court*, *pitch* or *track*.

1 **2** **3** **4** **5** **6**

track _____ _____ _____ _____ _____

4 Read and draw lines.

1 tennis **2** skiing **3** surfing **4** swimming

a I've got my goggles and I'm going to the pool.

b I've got my board and I'm going to the beach.

c I've got my racket and ball and I'm going to the court.

d I've got my goggles and my helmet, and I'm going to the mountains.

5 Choose, draw and write.

~~bat~~   board   goggles   helmet   net   racket

You need a bat for ...

baseball   table tennis   cricket

Make a *ball in the cup* game.

You need

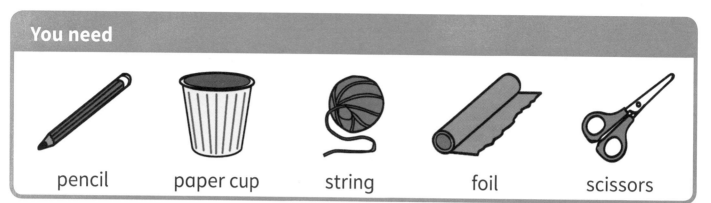

pencil   paper cup   string   foil   scissors

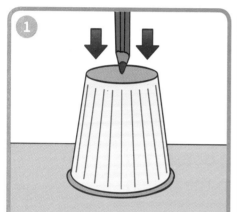

1 Make a hole in the bottom of the cup.

2 Put some string through the hole.

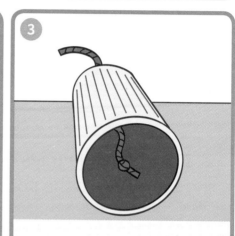

3 Tie a knot.

4 Make a foil ball at the end of the string.

5 Now play the *ball in the cup* game!

What do I know? 1 **Write and circle.**

1 I can write five sports.   **Yes / No**

badminton _____ _____ _____ _____

2 I like **ride / riding** my bike.

3

What do you like **do / doing**?

I like **play / playing** the guitar.

2 Look and write.

BIG QUESTION What do we need to play sports?

| track | helmet | net | ~~ball~~ | court | ~~pitch~~ |

ball   pitch   _____ _____   _____ _____

About me! 3 **Read. Then draw and write.**

I like listening to music.
Singing is fun.

1 Use the code to write the words.

Things to do this summer

1 **l e a r n** to swim

2 visit my c o u s i n s

3 take r i d i n g l e s s o n s

4 b u i l d a tree h o u s e

5 go c a m p i n g

6 go h i k i n g

7 r e a d a b o o k

8 h e l p in the g a r d e n

9 k e e p a s c r a p b o o k

Code

a = [briefcase]
b = [owl]
c = [butterfly]
d = [flower]
e = [guitar]
f = [palm tree]
g = [umbrella]
h = [tent]
i = [lizard]
k = [sailboat]
l = [cap]
m = [flip-flops]
n = [camera]
o = [pizza]
p = [ice cream]
r = [dolphin]
s = [starfish]
t = [sun]
u = [ice lolly]

1 Read and write.

go   build   take

(1) Can I _____ a tree house?

Yes, of course you can.

(2) Can I _____ riding lessons?

Yes, of course you can.

(3) Can we _____ fishing?

Yes, of course we can.

2 Look and write.

1 Can we g_____ h_____ ?   2 Can I g_____ c_____ ?

3 Write the words in the correct order.

1 we / cousins / our / Can / visit

Can we visit our cousins _____ ?

2 I / Can / to / learn / swim

_____ ?

3 scrapbook / a / I / Can / keep

_____ ?

4 help / garden / we / the / Can / in

_____ ?

1 🎧 037 🛡 **Can you remember? Listen and circle.**

(1) We all need a (holiday) / theme park
A time for play and rest.
(2) Sun and **tea** / **sea** – come with me,
Holidays are the best.

(3) Can we build a **tree house** / **sandcastle**?
Can we skip and run?
(4) Can we visit **grandparents** / **cousins**?
We want to have some fun.

(5) Can we **read a comic** / **ride a bike**?
Can we bake a cake?
(6) Can we **eat an ice cream** / **keep a scrapbook**?
We want to have a break.

2 🛡 **Write a new verse.**

Can we _____?   Can we _____?

Can we _____?   We want to _____.

1 Read and circle.

1 Does your brother like tennis?
   a Yes, he does.   b Yes, he is.   c No, he does.

2 How old is Lucy?
   a It's eight.   b November.   c She's seven.

3 Have you got a skateboard?
   a Yes, I am.   b No, I haven't.   c Yes, I can.

4 When do you get up?
   a At seven o'clock.   b Yes, I do.   c On the sofa.

5 Whose sock is this?
   a It's purple.   b It's mine.   c They're mine.

6 Where is the playground?
   a Between the school   b Yes, it's great.   c Behind the wardrobe.
     and the shops.

7 Would you like a kiwi?
   a Yes, I do.   b Yes, I can.   c No, thank you.

8 Are there any mangoes in the fridge?
   a Yes, there is.   b No, there are.   c Yes, there are.

2 **Look at the answers to Activity 1. Colour the boxes to find the hidden message.**

	1	2	3	4	5	6	7	8
a	w	o	n	l	c	o	r	a
b	z	a	l	k	d	i	t	o
c	s	e	m	j	b	u	n	e

The hidden message is: w_____ _____!

1 🎧 038 **Who says it? Listen and tick ☑.**

2 **What would they like to do? Read the story and draw lines.**

1 Flash would like to   build a treehouse.

2 Misty would like to   help her grandma in the garden.

3 Thunder would like to   visit her cousins.

3 **Look and write the numbers.**

1 Here you are, Grandma.

2 Can we come up?

3 And what would you like to do, Whisper?

1   **Who is working in a team? Look and tick ☑.**

2 🎧 039 **Listen and write the words under z or s.**

~~nose~~   house   **z**ebra   **s**wim   le**ss**on
li**z**ard   tenni**s**   tomatoe**s**

z		**s**	
nose			

3 🎧 040 **Listen, say and check your answers.**

1 **Look and read. Write the answers.**

1 Where are the boy and the girl?   in a **tree**

2 What is the boy wearing on his head?   a _____

3 What are they building?   a _____

4 Where are they now?   in the _____

5 What has the girl got in her hand?   a _____

6 Where are they now?   in the _____

7 How many sandwiches are there?   _____

Think and learn

Helping the environment

1 **Look and write.**

| natural environment | path | recycle | ~~recycling bins~~ | rubbish |

1 <u>recycling bins</u>

2 _____

3 _____

4 _____

5 _____

2 **How can we help the environment on holiday? Read and tick ☑.**

Do ...	Don't ...	
☑	☐	recycle your rubbish.
☐	☐	walk on the plants and flowers.
☐	☐	take your rubbish home.
☐	☐	play with the animals.
☐	☐	leave your rubbish on the ground.
☐	☐	walk on the path.
☐	☐	learn about the animals in their environment.

3 **What activities can we do? Look and write.**

build a sandcastle	go fishing	go hiking	go swimming
go climbing	look for shells	take riding lessons	take a photo

beach	mountains	lake
build a sandcastle		

4 **Choose, draw and write.**

| mountains | beach | ~~lake~~ |

At a lake, you can ...

go fishing

take a photo

go swimming

1   **Make a holiday mobile.**

You need

paper   scissors   pens   string   2 clean twigs   pencil

1

Draw four pictures of your favourite holiday activities.

2

Colour and cut them out.

3

Use a pencil to make a hole on top of each drawing.

4

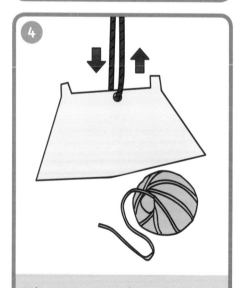

Tie some string to each picture.

5

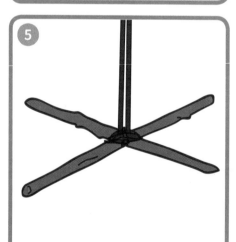

Tie the two twigs together.

6

Tie your pictures to the twigs to make your mobile.

What do I know?

1 **Write and circle.**

1 I can write five holiday activities. **Yes / No**

go hiking _____   _____   _____   _____

_____   _____   _____   _____

2 _____ we build a tree house?
Yes, of course you **can / can't**.

3 _____ I take riding lessons?
No, sorry. You **can / can't**.

BIG QUESTION **What makes a good holiday?**

2 **Read and circle.**

Have a good holiday and help the **(1)** **natural environment / rubbish** too.
Put your **(2)** **path / rubbish** in the **(3)** **recycling bin / rubbish**.
Walk on the **(4)** **natural environment / path** – not on the plants and flowers!

About me!

3 **Read. Then draw and write.**

My favourite holiday activity

is camping.

_____

_____

Back to school

floor   wall   crayon   bookcase   clock
window   cupboard   ~~board~~   chair   door

board

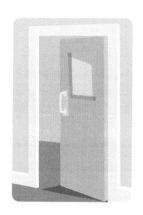

Back to school (continued)

sixty ~~ten~~ thirty ninety forty one hundred
seventy eighty fifty twenty

10 20 30

ten ________ ________ ________

40 50 60 70

________ ________ ________ ________

80 90 100

________ ________ ________

1 My day

get up   have dinner   get dressed   go to bed   go to school
have lunch   ~~brush your teeth~~   have breakfast   play in the park

brush your teeth

_____

_____

_____

_____

_____

_____

_____

_____

2 The zoo

polar bear   zebra   ~~bear~~   crocodile   snake
hippo   parrot   tiger   monkey

bear

_____

_____

_____

_____

_____

_____

_____

_____

swimming pool   park   hospital   café   playground
shop   train station   street   cinema   ~~bus stop~~   school

bus stop

4 The market

watermelons   potatoes   bread   eggs   greens
lemons   ~~beans~~   mangoes   kiwis   tomatoes   grapes

beans

5 My bedroom

sofa   poster   mirror   bed   rug
wardrobe   ~~armchair~~   table   lamp

armchair

_____

_____

_____

_____

_____

_____

_____

_____

nose   glasses   eyes   face   ~~cheeks~~
hair   chin   tears   mouth   ears

cheeks

_____

_____

_____

_____

_____

_____

_____

_____

_____

ship   taxi   bus   motorbike   ~~boat~~
scooter   skateboard   helicopter   lorry

_____

_____

_____

8 Sports club

basketball   ~~athletics~~   football   swimming   hockey
badminton   table tennis   volleyball   tennis   baseball

athletics

_____

_____

_____

_____

_____

_____

_____

_____

_____

Holiday plans

visit cousins   help in the garden   go hiking
learn to swim   read a comic   keep a scrapbook
take riding lessons   ~~build a tree house~~   go camping

build a
tree house

_____

_____

_____

_____

_____

_____

_____

_____